George W. Cable

The Busy man's Bible and How to Study and Teach it

.

George W. Cable

The Busy man's Bible and How to Study and Teach it

ISBN/EAN: 9783337225469

Printed in Europe, USA, Canada, Australia, Japan

Cover: Foto ©Suzi / pixelio.de

More available books at **www.hansebooks.com**

The Busy Man's Bible

AND

How to Study and Teach It

BY
GEORGE W. CABLE

MEADVILLE PENNA.
FLOOD & VINCENT
The Chautauqua-Century Press
1891

CONTENTS.

THE BUSY MAN'S BIBLE.

I.

WHY STUDY IT?

THE very essence of Christ's teaching is that religion is not a mere province of life, but the whole empire of life both in the individual and throughout human society. Everything that is right at all is, in so far, "good religion," and nothing is entirely right until it is "good religion." Religion is not to be grouped with, but comprises and appropriates, science, art, literature, commerce, handicraft, unskilled labor, sleep, recreative pleasures, and the furnishing of recreative pleasures. All these, be they essentials or only aids to life's fullest development, are but parts and phases of religion. Not merely must these things be done consistently with religion, and go side by side with a spirit of piety; nor are they merely among the things to be sanctified and saved; they are themselves parts of the work of saving the world.

Religion cannot be fairly called the doing of right things with right ends in view, unless it includes the great ultimate right end within its view and intention. And therefore to say we have no time to attend to "matters of religion" is to say we have no time to do anything in the right way. Religion is for men,—for busy men, for men busy in the affairs of the world, for men whose religious duty is to raise crops and herds, dig metals and minerals, make goods, sail ships, sell merchandise, write, edit, hold office, mold bricks, carry hods, sing, paint, and all the rest.

But religion is not all work any more than life is. It is "whatsoever we do." Eating and sleeping are among its duties; worship is among them in exactly the same way, for nourishment and refreshment. To work well one must eat and sleep; to eat and sleep well, one must work. Worship without work, work without worship, —either one will produce but a starved religion.

So, then, worship is for all, but especially for busy men. Hard fighters in the battle of life need the most and most nutritious food, both material and spiritual.

Now, many men have such a passion for the activities of life that they lose the faculty of rest and refreshment, and turn everything into work. Some sleep, but do not rest; some eat, but do not digest; and some worship, but get no spiritual nourishment, because their appetite craves and is satisfied with only the working parts and working phases of worship. Even if the activities they embrace are mental and studious, they only distend themselves with learning, though it may be in spiritual matters; and if their tastes are rather for administrative or executive affairs, you will find them "active and prominent in all kinds of church and Sunday-school work," and yet, visibly or invisibly, consciously or unconsciously, the victims of spiritual indigestion and insomnia, and, it may be, in far greater danger than they or we dream, of one of those strokes of moral apoplexy, which probably make among "active church-members" more defaulting

presidents and absconding cashiers than pure
hypocrisy makes. We busy men, whether in
the study, the field, or the counting-room, on
the exchange, the street, the unfinished building,
or the ocean, must see to it that we have strong
spiritual meat, and also a genuine spiritual digestion and assimilation, so that the strength of
Christ's word and example shall not fail to go
into all our judgment, all our desires, all our
will, and all our affections, and we not remotely
imitate, but potently assimilate and reproduce,
our Lord in all we do and are and seek.

Hence the large element of instruction in our
worship. If adoration is the wine, instruction
is the meat, of our spiritual repast. And the appetite and the digestion? They are study. The
spiritual birth may dispense with it; but the
spiritual growth and training can no more be
achieved in effective quantity and quality without it than can any other knowledge and training
which has been largely committed to the written
and printed page. A religious instruction limi-
ted to sermon and lecture hearing and Sunday-
school tradition is not enough. Taken alone, it

develops a rote religion which pre-empts the mind to the exclusion of a far better sort. True, study, in anything not a mere art or craft, is one of the best safe-guards, though even it is not a sure one, from rote education. What student of Scripture who has ever found by his own effort, hidden beneath the letter of the page, some truth which "flesh and blood have not revealed" unto him, can forget its transcendent power upon his spirit. We best relish and digest the game we have taken ourselves. The vulture eats, the eagle will not eat, the prey he did not himself catch. Luke accounted certain hearers "more noble than those of Thessalonica" in that even when Paul preached they "searched the Scriptures daily whether these things were so." And in our own day the busy men, of all men, need to do something of the same sort if they would not be spiritually dyspeptic.

II.

HOW TO BEGIN.

SAID a talented young man to a musician, "Tell me how to play the sonatas of Beethoven in their true spirit."

Said the musician, "You ask too much of me; yet—I will do what I can. What do you play these days?"

"Nothing."

"My friend! How shall I tell you how to play Beethoven when it is not your habit to play anything at all? To know how to play Beethoven you must first of all know how to play."

So with the Bible. To know how to study it, we must first of all know how to study.

Now, wrong notions of how to study are with-

out number, and probably every one of them
has been brought to the study of the Bible; but
one of the very worst not consciously dishonest
is the assumption that the Bible is not to be
studied as we study other books and other
things, but by a separate method all its own.
From the correct rendering of Beethoven or
Handel we do not look for the same musical results or mental effects as from Wagner or Rubin-
stein; yet we do not hesitate to bring to the
renderings of all these masters the same system
of notation, the same rules of harmony, the same
methods of execution. But for the Bible thousands of teachers and scholars claim an immu-
nity from fundamental methods of correct study,
without which we cannot get a firmly founded,
genuine conviction of the meaning and merits of
anything.

"Bring not your desecrating lines and plum-
mets, rules of building, or tenets of architectual
criticism, here," they cry; "this is the King's
palace." But in fact all the more because it is
the King's palace ought it to be tried and proved
by all these things; and in truth it is only when

we have so done that we can raise the confession from our own inmost souls, "This is the house of God; this is the gate of heaven."

"Doctor," once said a convalescent, "I'm no judge of books,—don't often read one; but I'm reading one now that seems to me a very fine book. I haven't noticed yet who wrote it, and I don't know how you'd pronounce its title; but it's something like I–van–hoe."

"My friend," said the physician, "I'd give large gold to be in your place long enough to be reading that book for the first time and not knowing who wrote it !"

Oh for the rare gift to come to the study of the Word of God as if strangers to men's claims for it, until its truth, sinking into mind and heart, establish its authority and convince us of its inspiration ! The true way to begin the study of all books is the true way for the Bible. Not in a spirit of carping unbelief, or of contempt or suspicion of our teachers; yet, in faithfulness to God, truth, and humanity, bearing in mind that things are not true because they are in the Bible, and cannot truly be Bible to us

until they would be just as true to us if they
were not in the Bible.

What! Shall we hold the Scriptures in dimin-
ished reverence? No; there need be no decrease
in the quantity of our reverence that may not be
immeasurably offset by increase in its quality.
An ounce of reverence founded on one's own
personal conviction and experience of Scripture
truth is worth in God's sight a hundredweight
of mere traditional reverence. Scripture truth;
—is the term a good one? Truth suffers every
time we put upon her the manacles of a limiting
adjective. Scripture truth, scientific truth, gos-
pel truth, practical truth! There is but one
kind of truth; and to it, wherever and however
found, we owe the solemn reverence we are prone
to give to the Bible as its greatest vehicle, instead of to itself.

But even this is not saying enough. Truth
itself, God's pure eternal truth, simply discov-
ered, observed, and emotionally reverenced, is
but treasure still buried. "The kingdom of
God cometh not by [mere admiring] observation"
—of it. Only as truth melts and runs into our

hearts, our lives, our daily conduct, and is there molded and coined into justice, righteousness, holiness, and universal love, do its latent powers become actual values. There cannot be even a correct approach to the study of truth, that regards truth or beauty as an ultimate and adequate end. All such studyings are, as to their spiritual value, but unfinished bridges ending in air, to be swept away by the first high wind of our intellectual pride, or the first high water of our physical appetites. Any real spiritual profit— nay, any permanent, potential conviction of truth—so got, is got without genuine credit to ourselves or our method, and, as it were, by lucky accident. Only the student who hungers and thirsts after righteousness shall be profitably filled.

If this be so, then how much less correct is an approach to the study of the Bible when prompted by the advance purpose to justify some theory of our own, orthodox or heterodox, or some belief of our church or of our social circle, or of our public community, concerning God's nature or man's duty. But when we think how much more of this kind of study than of any other has been given the Bible by the world, by the church, and by ourselves, and how much more of it the Bible has had to bear than any other book, we see a way in which the flippant old saying is true, about the Bible being "a fiddle on which you can play any tune you like." It was a pious monk who said, "Whoever seeketh an interpretation in this book shall get an answer from God; whoever bringeth an interpretation to this book shall get an answer from the Devil."

But it is not this error in its grossness as visibly practiced by others not of our sort that we need to be warned against; it is as it besets us, ourselves, an unseen, unfelt, subtle ailment, in our daily drawing near the oracles of God. The Bereans searched the Scriptures daily not to fortify, but to test, certain declarations of godly men. They sought not to prove that, but "to know whether," certain things were so.

The one only safe and sufficient motive to insure our correct approach to the study of God's Word is the desire to make ourselves and the world better. "Whosoever doeth my will shall "

—not merely know the doctrine; he "shall know of the doctrine whether it be of God."

III.

HOW TO STUDY.

NOW, supposing we have decided upon the right spirit in which to begin the study of the Bible, the fact still faces us that we cannot go on until we know the practical part of how to study. To study is an art. Besides a knowledge of its methods, it demands its own habitual practice. But this practice cannot be leaped into; it can only be gradually built up. One who has no habit of study, can no more rise up from a lecture on how to study the Bible, and go and put the method at once into practice, than if the lecture had been on how to play the harp or paint landscapes.

Take an extreme case. Here is a light, thoughtless, impatient, restless person. All his

or her powers of attention, memory, reflection,
and judgment, are in a state of disuse. Suddenly
something happens to arouse such a one to the
duty and privilege of studying God's Word; or,
better, he is siezed with a hunger and thirst
after righteousness, and, asking little about duty,
hastens to the Book of books. And behold! he
has not a single student's faculty developed.
We call this an extreme case; but is it unusual?
Look about over the whole mass of any average
adult church-membership. How many have the
habit of study? Or go farther. In the teaching
corps of any average Sunday-school, how many
are of a studious habit? Are they frivolous?
Not necessarily. Have they a light or heavy
contempt for books and learning? No; they
honor them. What then? Simply, they are of
and in the world's great common life, and are
habitually giving the lion's share of all their energies to the doing of things already long ago
thought out by others; they find no time and have
no acquired skill for inquiries, reflections, dis-
coveries, and genuing personal convictions, concerning things that belong to what they have

unluckily distinguished as the "domain of thought." We call them busy people,—as if others could not be as busy in mind as they are in body. They need to get somehow the habit of study, and have not noticed how much of the best of this habit they already have, though unapplied, nor how easily more of it may be got.

But we who give ourselves, and are generally given, credit as having this habit of study,—have we only the habit of studying books, or have we that vastly better gift, a studious habit of mind? For brains are so much better than books! And for our busy people there follows this welcome word: that it is only the habit of book study, and not the mere studious habit of mind, that taxes our time and leisure. Also, and better yet, that thousands who are too busy for book study are, in the few directions their minds take, more constant, diligent, genuine students, than thousands who, poring over books, have won the high degree of gold spectacles. The term "hard study" has got most lamentably entangled with the notion of printed pages, book-covers, and feats of memory; but when we substitute for it the nobler word, "hard thinking," we see how much of it there is, and how much more there might still be, in this great, busy world. We see how much of it there is good chance for, largely free from the time-devouring captivity of the student's desk and the late-glimmering lamp. True study is older than printing, or papyrus, or Moses' tables of stone.

We emphasize, then, these two points: First, the true spirit for the undertaking; the spirit whose incessant search is for truth, to turn it into holy being and lovely doing, and that proves, not truth from authority, but authority only from truth, and truth only from discernment and conviction in the mind and conscience of the inquirer himself; and, second, the true spirit for the method; the spirit that bids the mind be always diligent rather than docile; the spirit that weds a diligent mind to a docile heart; the spirit that values the studious mind above the study of books; the spirit of faithful, humble, hard thinking. Until we have in some degree possessed ourselves of these two essentials, this spirit for the undertaking and this spirit for the method, let us not say we know how to study the Bible.

IV.

BRAINS ARE BETTER THAN BOOKS.

IF books were nearly as good as brains, the estimates you and I once made of the prospective value of some of our schoolmates would not have been so faulty.

A. B. was a fellow of quick perception, you remember,—attentive, receptive, sympathetic, imitative, tractable, a lover of books and knowledge. To our astonishment, he has never given his generation a new thought,—hardly even an old thought in new dress. He will die never knowing that, with all his habit of study, he has never had a studious habit of mind. His mind is, and ever has been, all appetite, and no digestion. He never ruminates what he has browsed. He retains what he has acquired as sweet and undigested as a sealed tin can contains condensed milk.

C. D. was of quite another sort,—slow to comprehend, and seeming slower than he was, observant rather than attentive, . incredulous, unimitative, not too tractable, and amusingly distrustful of books. That fellow is to-day helping to widen the knowledge and mold the thought of his times. He had—what he scarcely realized, and what we quite overlooked—a studious habit of mind, a spirit of investigation and reflection, and that keen sense of perspective in his own correlation of facts which we call judgment. And best of all, he had—found out after school days were over—a rare gift of harmoniously subordinating the teachings of books to his ever-growing knowledge of things that books cannot teach. It pains many to know that he is not beyond a suspicion of being unorthodox. They have not proved the matter yet, either yea or · nay; for he shows no pride either of orthodoxy or heterodoxy. And they are rather afraid to try; for they might succeed, and then they would not know what to do with him next.

What we seek here to emphasize is, not the

great value of mere intrepidity or originality of thought. "Seek earnestly the best gifts,"—but originality is only very good, not best. To prize it unduly is a species of moral giddiness,—a palpable vanity. Our point is, not originality, but the virtue and grace of modestly using and prizing brain more than book.

A young lady, teaching in a mission Sunday-school in one of our Southern cities, had told a pupil—a big, grimy, short-haired athlete, older than she—that God can do everything. By and by, when she was getting well away from this, to her, axiomatic starting-point, he asked: "Say, teacher, d–d'you say God can do everything?"

"Yes."

"Well, say, teacher, can God make a rock so big 'at he can't lift it?"

That teacher's easy life had allowed her the chance to "study"; the pupil's rude lot had shut him up to hard thinking. Hard knocks, we may guess, had forced him into the habit of questioning and reflecting before everything he was asked to believe. The moment the assertion of God's omnipotence was laid upon his tongue, he began a mental mastication of it, to reduce it to reasonable and intelligible conditions before swallowing it. We can pay no higher homage to truth, in the Bible or out of it, than modestly but faithfully to hold it in suspense until we can give it, not a mere unquestioning assent, but the cordial testimony of our own sincerest intelligence. This is all the more our duty and advantage because truth is easy to digest in exact proportion to its moral value. The few truths absolutely vital to salvation do not have to be chewed at all; they are the sincere milk of the word,—or, let us say, of the cocoanut, which some would have us swallow whole, and spit the shells up afterward if we can.

But this plan of using brain more than book is not only virtue and grace, it is also opportunity. We can carry this habit with us daily and hourly, as we cannot carry books. Consider, in this land so teeming full of men almost too busy to read the newspaper, what swarms of them have found they can, and for worldly gains' sake must and do, keep up through almost every waking hour a diligent thinking, questioning, reflecting, calculating, recapitulating, reconsidering, deciding! Thousands of just such declare and believe they would study the Bible if they could only—as to time and method—see how to do it. Let them simply give a seventh or tenth of that hard daily and hourly thinking which they give to their business, to the plainest utterances of the Bible upon God's nature and man's duty, and they will gain more knowledge and spiritual refreshment than by poring with eager receptiveness and docile assent over whole commentaries. They will get less learning, it may be, but more wisdom.

And so I make bold to say, when you do sit down to study Scripture, dispense, or at least try to dispense, from the beginning, with commentaries and the various other forms of lesson-helps.

What! At the very start? Yes; rather then than later. Book-helps oftener narcotize than stimulate our own thought. They make us think we are thinking, when we are only locking step with the thought of some one else. Even when they help us to think, they are apt to make thinking too easy. Easy thinking yields but flimsy thought.

V.

COGITATION FIRST—COMMENTATORS LAST.

BUT shall one set himself above the finest scholarship of the day and of the ages? Not at all. Does the lad or lass in school set himself above his preceptor because he toils alone with slate and arithmetic, and seeks aid only in extremity? All lesson-helps should be as banks and bankers to our minds in our spiritual commerce with the Bible; that is, to be called on for aid always with a certain sparingness, and not at all until, as we may say, our own thinking powers have built up for themselves a respectable credit.

But would you have every Tom, Dick, and Harry with a mind of his own? No. I wish I could. Even then all men would not think differently.

Men are gregarious in thought as well as in bodily activities. Like conditions in and about us make us like-minded. The form and spirit of the civil government under which we happen to live, the degree of industrial, civil, political, or private social liberty we happen to enjoy, powerfully mold our reasonings about God and duty, and threaten to make us the characterless results of our accidental surroundings, unless we labor to cultivate those individual powers of thought and moral convictions and resolve, without which our religion brings small honor to God, poor strength to our own souls, and scant profit to mankind.

Some one will say, "Why not, for this very danger of being shaped wholly by our own surroundings, put ourselves promptly under the tutelage of the commentators?" No! We should thus escape the domination of our own surroundings only to fall captive to the conditions that surrounded the commentators. What those conditions were, read in history, and shudder. The commentators of the past are of a past the most of which the Christian world hopes never to return to. Had they had the light of our day, many a page of theirs would never have been written, and few indeed would be just what they are.

As for the commentators and lesson-helps of to-day, take, for instance, the one you are using right now for the " preparation "—what a word—what a process—to substitute for genuine study—for genuing thinking ! the "preparation" of next Sunday's lesson: Do you know from what older fountains of merely human argument and purpose, or how largely from them, the fountain from which you are drinking is fed ? Oh, put the lesson-help aside ! Rub out your copied sums from the tablet of your mind and heart, and start again with nothing but the Bible and a clean slate,—as clean as you can make it from whatever thought, right or wrong, Athanasius or Augustine, Luther, Calvin, Loyola, Milton, Bunyan, Wesley, Fenelon, or Coleridge, may have uttered. Don't be afraid of your own originality; there's no strong chance that you have enough of it to be afraid of. Get an answer from your own soul. Be it right or

wrong, a shout or a whisper, get it from yourself. Then—to press the school-room figure—
bring your slate to the class; look into the commentators and lesson-helps of past and present
with dilligence, with caution, with humility,
and with hunger and thirst after righteousness
"prove all things, hold fast that which is good."

One more limitation: We can never make a
very intelligent or even safe use of books or traditions about the Bible until we know something
of whence, how, and wherefore, as well as from
whom, such books or traditions originated. We
should want the history of doctrines, and not
any mere personal or ecclesiastical sanction of
them.

We need as Bible students to know concerning
important theories about God and goodness
whether they have been truly drawn from the
Bible or only thrust into it by the bias of some
person or nation or age or exigency of politics
or ecclesiastics. And we can know. Histories
of these things are neither scarce nor unwieldy
nor dry. Even a "business man," keeping the
book somewhere in sight, and taking a little

dip into it once a day or twice a week, or giving it a single hour on each of a few Sundays, may read such invaluable helps to the study of Scripture as Principal Tulloch's "Religious Thought in Great Britain in the Nineteenth Century," or Professor Allan's "Continuity of Christian Thought."

We say this to those who read few books and have no habit of book study; who do not propose to become learned in the deep theories of religious philosophers; who do not ask how to study even the Bible with the notion that to study the Bible is in itself a virtue,—but who seek to study it as one of the very best means known for learning how best to love and obey God, and love and serve mankind. We do not escape the theories of religious philosophers by remaining ignorant of their origin and history; we only wear their shakles unconsciously. To read one or two historical surveys of this sort is a wonderful emancipation from an unquestioning and therefore ignoble subjection to the Scripture interpretations of ages darker than our own. Yet mark; to read even such books instead of the Scriptures, or in any way to give them precedence over the Scriptures, is to show not how, but how not, to study the Bible.

All our study of the Bible, with or without books, should give us a result within ourselves independent of books at last, and from first to last should be faithful, diligent thinking,—a thinking unceasingly centered upon the problem, How more and more clearly and fully day by day to achieve in all our being, not Scripture lore, but the likeness—and to apply in all our doings the principles—of Jesus Christ our Lord.

VI.

COMPARE WATCHES.

WE must not yield ourselves blindly to the written thought of ages past, nor drift supinely upon whatever current of thought of our own day we may happen to be caught by. But, on the other hand, we must not, as students, indulge ourselves in a self-sufficient and persistent privacy and isolation. The truth is that cluster of grapes which the spies brought out of the valley of Eshcol. No one man could carry it without damage or loss. But one man thrust his staff among its stems,—maybe that staff was a lesson-help,—"and they bare it upon a staff between two." I wonder if those two were not Caleb and Joshua; for they were just the kind who would rather surrender some liberty and go yoked thus to each other, than bring a mangled and bleeding truth to their fellows camped in the wilderness.

No one man is tall enough or broad enough to carry the whole truth without dragging it in the dust. We need to be almost constantly testing the correctness of our own convictions of truth, righteousness, and goodness by a generous consideration of the convictions of those round about us both near and far, both like and unlike. We need not be servile; we need not be unstable; we need not be rashly or weakly impressionable; our aim need not—must not—be uniformity; it must be the elimination of error; our establishment as nearly as possible in absolute truth for absolute righteousness' and lovliness' sake. Our judgments—even our consciences—are watches for the keeping of truth instead of time; and sometimes their hands catch. It is one of the strongest reasons for the organic grouping of God's servants in the church form, that to study the Bible best we must study it much in friendly concert, seeking neither confirmation nor contradiction more than its opposite;

but taking both with the same modest, kindly, thoughtful caution and courage; differing whenever, but only when, we must; differing, but not dividing. There is nothing like that to save our notions of God and duty from fantastical and mischievous distortions.

We repeat: that we must, first, last, and always, make our study of the Bible a search for absolute truth back of all assertion; for absolute right back of all will and authority; for absolute duty back of all exigency or commandment, and of supreme spontaneous goodness back of and above all questions of duty? Our Bible study should not always be a short search; but always it should be a search for the shortest, simplest way to our best possible understanding and practical acceptance of these things. Not be strong in the Bible, but "be strong in the Lord."

The unconscious method even of great thinkers has too often been to start with certain preconceptions of what was right or necessary for the establishment or maintenance of some system of ecclesiastical order, conservative or progressive; to model upon this their conceptions of God's nature, and from such conceptions to draw their definitions of man's duty to himself, his fellows and his race, using the Bible from beginning to end, not to determine, but only to fortify, their positions. If great and holy men have fallen into this error, how much more may we do so unless we take heed how we study the Bible.

But the fault would be immeasurably greater in us than in them if we should follow their missteps. They, even in and through their error, were ahead of their age; but we, repeating it, can only be behind ours. Wherefore let us see to it that in studying the Scriptures we draw not our theology from our politics, and our morals from our theology; but our theology from the noblest morals we can find in the Bible, and our politics from our theology.

But by this method see what more we gain: The *moral* intent and value, in every page and text of Scripture, become naturally the primary and paramount consideration. For those we search, and finding those according to the best measure of our moral perceptions, we exchange

Calvin's solicitude for Luther's comparative unconcern as to whether Moses wrote the Pentateuch, or Paul the Epistle to the Hebrews. Questions of authorship, discrepancies of text, apparent historical inaccuracies, seeming contradictions of our scientific knowledge, whether this page is poetry or history, or another is legend or fact, are matters we can commit to professional scholars, or our own later leisure. The mind— the spirit—that has accustomed itself to see that the fundamental truth and essential part of any sincere utterance remains potentially the same whether its literary form be mythus, legend, allegory, poetry, song, drama, romance, philosophy, or history, has learned the most important single thing that can be learned of how to study the Bible. This will lead to another noble thing.

VII.

THE RIGHT SPIRIT IS NINE-TENTHS OF THE RIGHT METHOD.

WHAT we come to the Bible for when we come rightly is not rules of life. What, not even them? No; we come for principles of life, not rules. Alas! it is still our lower man that is speaking when we ask to be driven in harness by rules, instead of following, unharness-ed, the beckoning guidance of principles. The essence of Christian conduct is to rise beyond the schoolmastership of rules and commandments into the fulfilment of principles and precepts, where duty is swallowed up in an understanding choice and an all-embracing love. Rules are like the boundary lines we lay along the surface of the ground to part our lot or field from that of our neighbor; but principles are like that solemn clause in the wording of Spanish land-titles, which gives the holder ownership and do-mination "from the heavens to the center of the earth." This is the way we must seek to own a moral truth. It must be ours not merely along and between fixed lines on a certain tract of earth; but ours from the throne of God to the center of our corporate being.

Now two things are essential to our real ownership of a moral truth. Whatever else we may fail to understand about it, we must under-stand its absolute righteousness; and we must give it the consent of our affections and wills. To call a thing right without feeling it right, is wrong. To try to feel it right merely because it has been called right, is to yield that homage to authority which God has nowhere given us any right to yield to anything but that which we see to be true and right.

And here we are put in mind that some truths in the Bible are worth vastly more than others, both for their essential importance and for the degree of our ability truly to possess them. The truth is worth nothing to us merely for being in the Bible. Its value begins with and is bounded by our spiritual discernment of it; not a consciousness of some supernatural operation, but a discernment that enlists the consent of our whole spirit, and no more depends any longer on whether the rest of mankind believe or deny it than if God had spoken it to us audibly out of the sky. Spiritual experience is authority. "Blessed art thou, Simon Bar-jona"—and— "The truth shall make you free."

Still, Bible students will say, "Give us rules. To give us only principles takes us by surprise. · We yearn for rules; a few, at least. Give us a method." Very well.

Bring to the study of the Bible such habits of study as belong to your particular daily life. Are you an employee? You give studious consideration to all your employer's orders and instructions. You observe minutely their letter; but you do so, not to evade, but the more surely to understand and execute, their spirit; and you decide the spirit of any particular order by the spirit of his whole business. You view his commands very practically. Your study of them is not speculative or controversial; it is always to know what to do, how to behave! Bring that habit of study to God's and God's prophets' orders and instructions. Are you an employer? Have you a large and important business correspondence? Then you are a laborous student whenever you open your mail. You have to discern the exact intent, as far as you can, of each and every epistle. Now and then one puzzles you. Then you try to put yourself as far as you may into its writer's place. You call in all the knowledge you can get from others to help you to a conclusion, yet just as diligently you see to it that you catch no false bias from them, or accept their conclusions without truly making them your own. You beware, too, of all inelastic rules of interpretation. You also keep down your own self-assertion. You put away all ingenious constructions. And so you read and weigh, and read and weigh. Do so with the Bible.

Study, we say again, is a kind of eating. If your mind has not eaten much for a long time, feed lightly, but often. Line upon line. Three lines a day are far better than twenty-one lines once a week. Yet remember the Bible is no mere wood-pile, from which to draw a fagot or an armful at random. It is a structure. Enter in by its door. Never take up a book of the Bible to study it, or any part of it, without studying first the great main subject and motive of the book. To consider to whom, and specifically for what, it was written, is of more worth than to know by whom it is written. Never lose sight of these as you press on into the study of its parts.

Never be content with an understanding of less than the eternal moral principle underlying the narrative or discourse, and its practical bearings on your own life. Push for these as a storming party pushes for the citadel, not stopping on the right hand or on the left to gather intellectual booty. Never conclusively call an interpretation of God's Word your own because your church or mine declares or denies it, but only when you could not help but call it your own if all the churches on earth forbade it. Yet remember the church is your teacher and your mother. Jesus Christ is her husband. May you be such a student of his holy Word that others, seeing your good works, may glorify our Father in heaven.

VIII.

LAPPING AS A DOG LAPPETH.

BUT, now, how is the "busy man"—that man the work of whose life and religion is not, and cannot be, Bible-study—to pursue enough Bible study to insure him spiritual nourishment? First of all, he has got to class it with sleeping and eating among life's genuine and daily necessities. He must have his daily "fifteen minutes for refreshment" in spiritual things.

We will assume, then, that he sets apart that much time on every work-day, say at bedtime or on rising, and that to this he adds one hour on Sunday without sacrificing church attendance or Bible class. To avoid neglecting the matter, he knows that he must have a fixed meal-time for his spiritual repast. Let us suppose his Sunday hour is in the afternoon or evening. Two sermons are sometimes better than one, but one with an hour of Bible study is better than two without it.

In almost any case the International lessons are the best line of study for him to follow. The busy man is kept in view in their selection and treatment. They have a current literature, and are accommodated to the plan of transient daily study. All the weekly religious journals treat them, and the various quarterlies cost but five cents each. But—supposing you to be the "busy man," and the Sunday hour to have come—be warned once more; do not begin the lesson's study in any sort of "lesson-help." Don't cry "help" till your strength fails. Go straight to the Scripture text itself. Helps will be good by and by, not to give us first conceptions, but to supplement and confirm our right conceptions and correct our wrong ones.

Read the Scripture text of the lesson carefully, with as much context as may be needed to make the meaning of the passage as plain as context

can. Then read the text again, slowly and with
great scrutiny. Read it aloud, distributing the
emphasis with your best accuracy; this often
sheds a sudden flood of light upon the page, and
meanings that have been hiding away persist-
ently start from cover at sound of a voice. Read
again, noting marginal readings. Read again in
the Revised Version. Read again. Sooner or
later, this rubbing will bring out a new lustre.
Note the lesson's time, place, circumstances, per-
sonages, their relations to each other, etc.; but
do not let these or any other by-paths carry you
far from the main road. You are a busy man,
seeking food and refreshment. Seek the vital,
practical truth of the lesson. Try to find some
central idea for which the passage seems to have
been written. So found, it will be worth ten
times as much as if found, without search, in a
lesson-help. But do not be fanciful; do not be
ingenious. Seek out the great simplicities of the
science, art, and practice of living: "the way,
the truth, the life." Try to simplify truth.
You can never be sure that truth is truth until
it is simple. The doctrines of first importance

are all simple; what cannot be simplified is not of first importance; put it to one side. Christ never made the essentials of his religion hard to understand.

You use, of course, a reference Bible. Do not try to look out all the references; but if there is any parallel passage, read and compare it carefully with the lesson text. Thus your hour will be consumed. Yet the passage may refuse to yield any new light or inspiration, and as you push aside your book or books, and rise from the task, you wonder at the committee's choice of this lesson. Hence it is well to know that much harder, more experienced, and notedly successful students often have the same trouble with lessons that nevertheless turn out at length to be the very richest in their yield. The new light this lesson is to shed may delay its coming until near the end of the week.

Meanwhile, here are fifteen minutes of each day in which to pursue the subject. In them we turn to lesson-helps. Almost all of these give a list of Scripture readings bearing on the subject of the following Sunday's lesson, one for each day. Read one each day, but with it read the lesson itself. Give what is left of the fifteen minutes daily to a careful use of the lesson-help. So the week wears around.

One more suggestion, where a great many must be withheld for the sake of brevity: It is good, in the early weeks of a quarter, to read, each week-day morning, in place of the reading selected by the lesson-help, two of the twelve Sabbath lessons in the series of the quarter, in their order of time. Thus we may come into understanding of, and harmony with, the sacred writer's intention, gain and hold a general oversight of our field of inquiry, and avoid that fragmentary treatment which dwarfs so much—nearly all—lay Bible study.

On Sunday morning you come to Bible class. What has been gained? First, you have found that you can "find time to look at the lesson," just as women, as soon as they feel the necessity, find time to read the newspaper. Next, you have, with a minimum of labor, aggregated an amount of week-day study to which you could not have given ninety minutes continuously, nor forty-five, any day in the whole work-week. And then you have taken your spiritual bread in the best way for its effectiveness as, so to speak, tonic and nourishment. And at length you meet your class-leader in the class hour, not "with the lesson prepared,"—every hour in the week would not be enough for that; it is a bottomless deep,—but with yourself somewhat prepared for the lesson, and the leader enabled to teach you twice, thrice, four times as much as he could if you came to get your first impressions from him. If he cannot, you may suspect him of having "glanced over the lesson" for the first time a half-hour before the time for meeting his class: If so, quit him ! Find one who can teach you something, or else become a teacher yourself. Men fully as busy as you manage to do it, and grow in grace by it. So can you or I.

And now, as to teaching.

IX.

PROVE THE BOOK BY TRUTH, NOT TRUTH BY THE BOOK.

THEY say of some hardy shrubs that one may take them and invert them, planting their branches in the ground and leaving their roots outspread in the air, and the roots will become leafy and fruitful branches and the branches will become roots, so like are the two in their essential nature. So like each other are study and teaching. Nothing has been amply studied till we feel we can teach it; and no teaching can keep its due freshness and energy once the teacher ceases to be a student. The right kind of study is a teaching oneself, and the right kind of teaching, especially of such inexhaustible themes as those of the Bible, is mainly a studying with others.   To know truly how to study the Bible will itself show us how to teach it.

And this can never be rightly by a system and method all the Bible's own.   As in its study, so in its teaching, we must recognise and follow the great general principles of the twin arts of studying and teaching any and all things; the very first of which is that all sorts of truth are one sort at last and that the only competent and final authority of truth and right is conviction in the mind and conscience of him to whom it is addressed.   It is a sad perversion of the true art of teaching, and saddest when the things taught are those of the Bible, for a teacher, either directly or by implication, to ask his pupils to pay assents and consents in advance of convictions imparted.   The Bible is not itself the truth. Grant that it is, somehow as no other book is, God's book, and that he made it; yet God did not make truth any more than he created himself; and that teacher is far astray who accepts and teaches moral truth because it is in the Bible instead of accepting and teaching the

Bible because he ever more and more finds it the richest, purest vehicle of moral truth on earth. Hence this for a rule: Keep your teaching concentrated upon those few great simple truths to the understanding and acceptance of which books and scholarship are only aids, not essentials.

There are those who claim that certain fundamental and preliminary truths must be accepted and taught on the pure authority of the Bible or we cannot begin to teach the Bible at all.

Suppose a case. I bid a new pupil open the scriptures and read:

" 'In the beginning God created' "—He stops. What is the trouble?

"I do not believe there is a God."

What ought I to reply; that he must begin with that belief or we cannot begin at all? His blood would be on my head. No, I should say,

"Never mind that now; a great many men fancy they entirely and incessantly believe there is no God; and a great many who fancy they entirely and incessantly believe God is, have not even found out that such a belief is a thing of de-

grees.   Those who entirely and incessantly either
believe or disbelieve in God are rare.   The men
whose minds were never shaken with doubts
did not write the Psalms.   Thoroughly and constantly to believe that 'God is and is the re-
warder of them that dilligently seek him,' is a
great achievement and this book offers to show
that to do so is a possible and blessed thing.
Let us open it reverently"—

He interrupts: "Why should I reverence a
book whose very first word I am not ready to
accept?"

What shall I answer! Shall I try to show
him how unreasonable he is! No, I will say,
"Never mind reverence for the *book* just yet.
You have abundant reverence for truth, have
you not?"

"Abundant!" he replies.

I doubt it; but I only say, "Well, we will
read on a little way and see if, right here on this
first leaf, involved in a narrative of some sort,—
no matter just what sort right now,—we do not
find one of the richest treasuries of moral truth
ever written or printed on one book leaf by the

hand of man. We shall see whether the kind of God here described or implied is one whose existence and nature it is worth while to consider any farther." And so we begin again.

Conviction first, creed afterward. From his own experience a friend tells me this: He met on the highway travelling on horseback, as he was, and in the same direction, a stranger, but one known to him as an irascible and violent skeptic. Said he, by and by, "Well, as the Bible says"—

It was a red rag to the other. "I don't believe the Bible!—No, not 'some things in it' either!—Not a line!—Not a word!—No, I don't! Name it! name anything in that book that I believe; I defy you!"

"Why, my friend, you believe 'A soft answer turneth away wrath.'"

"Yes, I do."

"Well, hereafter read the Bible for what you *already believe in it.* You will be astonished to find what a large and precious part that is of the whole book and of every portion of the whole book. That is mainly what the whole book was written for."—They went their several ways.

Years afterward, journeying in the same region, this chance teacher of an hour on the highway found his pupil a devout and active member of the church of Christ. He had proved the Bible by truth, not truth by the Bible. Hundreds of us unconsciously satisfy ourselves with trying to teach the Bible, instead of simply using the Bible to teach christianity.

X.

TEACH THE CHRIST-LIFE.

STUDYING or teaching, it is one; the pursuit of truth or beauty for mere truth or beauty's sake is a vain mistake of means for ends. The end of Bible teaching is not only not the Bible, it is not even truth or beauty; not even the beauty of holiness. It is the impartation to —nay, better, it is the development of, truth— all kinds of truth—in the pupil's daily conduct, and of all kinds of beauty in his character. The end of all true Bible teaching—we all know it; the only trouble is to remember it—and not the ultimate end alone, but the immediate end every time we sit down to it—is the development of a better likeness of Christ in the pupil's conduct and character. This and this only is what I mean by teaching christianity.

This is what I mean by using the Bible to teach christianity. Not a headlong attempt to show Christ manifestly set forth in every page and paragraph; that would be trying to begin at the top to mount Jacob's ladder: Not the cramming of final, crowning truths of christianity into parts of scripture that do not really contain them; distorting the Bible to teach christianity: Not contriving allegoric or symbolic meanings and then swamping and sinking them with eager and far-fetched moralizings; drowning the Bible to teach christianity: Not expanding, even in studying the apostolic writings, upon the ever-so-valuable non-essentials that accompany christianity, as if they were parts of its essence. The true use of the Bible is none of these. Its true use in a teacher's hands is for him the better to maintain that all truth, all beauty, are parts of christianity, and finding whatever truth and beauty are really contained in the page before him, to relate and adapt them accurately, faithfully, and with all skillful despatch, to christianity's only one or two supreme essentials.

So we say once more, whatever the book of scripture, whatever the passage, whatever momentary indirection may be necessary, the end always in sight, the battle standard, the goal in the race, must be the inculcation of practical christianity. We must not say *make* all things bear to that point, but *use* everything only and always as it does naturally bear to that point; and where it does not, hasten by. Moreover, we must labor to hold the pupil as steadfastly to the same effort. Whatever arises in either the teacher's or the pupil's mind, let it be met by the challenge, as of a gentle gatekeeper,—what can you tell us of practical christianity?

There are ways of teaching the Bible that leave christianity untaught; the Bible is not christianity; christianity is at least as much older than the Bible as Enoch is. The Bible, even if every separate word of it be divinely inspired is only christianity's revelation, the tree that bears christianity. The words of Christ, hanging from that tree, are its fruit. But it also bears christianity in all its parts; for christianity is its all-pervasive essence; and whatever part of the Bible we teach, be it root, bark, sapwood, heart, leaf, flower, fruit or seed, our constant, preeminent, diligent purpose should be, must be, to extract from it by the distilling power of thought and converse, the eternal truths of christianity and turn them into duty, conscience and choice. The Bible, christianity, even Christ himself, are but flint to us, not fire, save as they kindle in us the pure flames of justice, mercy and love. No follower of Christ may hope to profit any soul to whom he teaches the Bible except when he so teaches it as to widen and in-tensify the Christ-life in the affections and daily actions of his learners. This is the whole final purpose of the Bible. Whenever we do not in some degree accomplish this we do not succeed in really teaching the Bible at all. And since every counterfeit sort of Bible-teaching is easier than this sort, we should make this sort our par-amount purpose each time we sit or stand to teach, and from the moment we begin, to the end.

XI.

DON'T DISCOURSE—AND DON'T DOGMATIZE.

IF the noblest and most indispensable part of real study is not hard study, but hard thinking, then our Bible-teaching must be of a kind that will never tend to lull, but always to stimulate the pupil's own pondering and questioning energies. Here lie the great danger and small value of the lecturing or discoursing habit in the Bible teacher. Better any ten sincere words from any pupil, the result of his own thought, than a hundred from his teacher that do not excite the pupil to think for himself.

"I know my lesson." How many millions of times has that been said untruly! We know our lesson not when we have memorized its text or merely accepted its statements in passive credence, but when we have distinguished in it what to us is positively knowable and have made it our own positive knowledge; have weighed what to us is believable and made it our own personal belief; and recognising also whatever in it is to us not yet absolutely knowable or even fixedly believable, but only good to hope for, have taken it into our hopes.

One who knows a lesson thus can teach it; and you may know a good Bible teacher by seeing him often playing pupil to his pupils and bidding them teach him. Thus is developed, in both teacher and taught, the skill to distinguish with a hale, sane readiness and self-candor between the many good things that some as yet can only hope, the fewer that may be fully believed, and that great few which can be, and need to be, absolutely known. A class so taught will not often be found spending on minor questions time out of proportion to their comparative values. I can imagine such a class saying, "With Paul we hope in the resurrection; with David, the prophets, apostles and martyrs, we *believe* in God; but we *know*—absolutely, by our own lives, we *know*—that every sin is so much death. We *know* that Christ's righteousness, holiness and unselfish, yearning love, as far as we succeed in repeating them in our own hearts and activities, are even now and here eternal life and joy, eternal in breadth whatever they may be in length. And we *know* that the better we can learn and apply these the stronger will be our real belief in God, the surer our faith in his goodness and mercy, and the brighter and nobler our hope in the resurrection.

XII.

STUDY THE PUPIL.

WE must help our pupils to think for themselves. Yet while we teach them that only by their own thought and desire they can truly reach the great ultimate conclusions necessary to the soul's salvation, the teacher's great office remains, to smooth the way and shorten the journey to those conclusions. On one hand the skillful teacher will—not minutely, but largely—accomodate himself and his teaching to the natural qualities and tendencies of the particular pupil's mind. To emotional and imaginative temperaments he will ever be holding forth that a heart which ignores the head is forgetting its marriage vows; while to unsusceptible and argumentative natures he will keep it ever in view that the citadel of the soul is not the head, but the heart. Hence on the other hand, whatever the temperament with which he is dealing he will remember that the heart is the objective point, and that be the pupil of what sort he may, it is a hundred times easier to get the essentials of christianity into his head by way of his heart than into his heart by way of his head.

The careful teacher will also duly adapt his teaching to the pupil's earlier training and preconceptions. Where he finds a pupil's notions of God's nature and methods and of man's duties and destiny poorer and lower than his own, he will begin there to build better before he hints of destroying what has been faultily built. Every soul is a ship in a storm, and a wise commander will slip no anchor-chain because it is too weak, until a stronger has fully taken its place and made the weaker only an encumbrance.

XIII.

SIMPLIFY.

BUT even while he is doing this a wise teacher will not fail to teach also that the largeness and accuracy of the christian's notions of God and duty, important as they are, are not the sheet anchor of his hope. That anchor, he will teach, is a far simpler thing; it is his heart's acceptance of God's mercy, authority and love. What a parable was that great storm a year or so ago in Apia bay. There, when every anchor dragged, the captain of one ship the great engine heart of which was strong enough to make his purpose good, slipped his anchors, and as he passed the helpless *Trenton*, shouted to her commander, "I am going out to sea!"—went, and rode out on the open deep the storm that filled the harbor with wrecks. So may the wise Bible teacher teach, that when our best notions of God and duty fail us like dragging anchors on a bad anchorage, the contrite soul with all its doubts may still cast itself upon the boundless sea of the Divine love and find safety and peace.

The effort of the wise teacher will be ever toward the completer simplification of God's truth and salvation's terms. He will never lead downward into the darkness of the Bible's obscurities; he will ever be leading upward into the lights of its great simplicities. He will never treat a pupil's sincere doubt with resentment, contempt, or any other form of unkindness; and he will treat every doubt as sincere until it is glaringly proved not to be so.

He will teach that there are more things in the Bible that one need not try to rescue from all doubt than most persons admit there are. And he will teach his pupils the very best use of doubts; which is, to turn us ever back to the few great things that cannot be doubted, and to the priceless things which we learn to believe by wisely acting as if we believed them. Some doubts may be even best left unsettled. Where, for instance, a doubt is a mere hesitation between varying interpretations of a Scripture passage, he will teach each pupil to hold fast to whatever he finds good in each and all of them and to put aside without fear, as without pride, whatever is not.

✠

XIV.

THE PUPIL'S OWN SAKE.

LET us not run into a multitude of good rules. When one asks for rules I seem at once to see and hear a thousand of them filling the atmosphere about the poor teacher's head, buzzing and threatening, but finding no central, sovereign, queen-bee truth to swarm upon, and I feel that there must be some one transcendent formula wanting to the art of teaching, which no one yet has found. I search vainly in others' counsel and in my own mind for this undiscovered truth, this absent keystone, and such poor success as I can pluck from the thorny tangle of my mistakes and failures I seem to get—as far as method is concerned—by believing in the existence of such a supreme principle and in still seeking though never finding it.

Principle, I say; not rule. Rules are risky things, soon worn out, easily spoiled, and, however good, bad as soon as they obscure our view of principles. A principle, I say; but just where or what it is I cannot surely tell. I can only suggest one or two thoughts more that seem to me to point the direction which our search for this great heart-truth of the whole art of Bible-teaching ought to take.

One of these is the thought that we should teach always visibly and supremely in the pupil's personal interest; not supremely in society's, nor the Bible's, nor the church's—neither our own church's nor the church's universal—nor even supremely in our Lord Christ's interest, save as he has made his interest identical with that of every human soul. If on a certain ship only one man could be sent as missionary to heathen lands, and two were eager to go, and each seemed as fit as the other, and our Lord himself were bodily present to choose between them, and should ask each one why he so yearned to go, and the first should answer, "For thy sake,

Lord," and the second answer, "Lord, for the heathen's own sake," verily the second would be his first choice.

To apply this principle successfully, to teach always visibly and absorbingly in the pupil's personal interest, there is but one way. That is to love the pupil; not merely to love his soul— that phrase is too often a cheat and a snare; but to love the whole pupil's every true interest, even as Christ loves ours. If we cannot begin our teaching with such love, if for a time only "the love of Christ constraineth us," yet let that move us dilligently to make ourselves love our pupils, few or many, in general and in particular, all and singular. If we can begin no better we can at least act out the love we only wish we felt; acting it out not in mere manners, but in acts and works lovingly and lovably performed, which by impulse we would do only for those we love.

And this sort of teaching need not at all take the form or spirit of any mischevious concession to the pupils' selfishness. Let this thought inform it: That this universe is a great unit. It is not a mere aggregation, it is a vast harmony. Whenever, wherever, whatever, in science, art, history, letters, morals, government or handicraft we set about to teach, we ought, it seems to me, to make it plain in the very start that we are about to consider an integral, inseparable part of all things. I fancy I could so delight a little child with some pictueresque account of the great world of knowledge to which the alphabet is one key that he would not rest until he had learned how to turn that key in its lock.

I might find much trouble to attract the attention and interest of a pupil, young or old, to the matter I wish him to consider; but keeping practically in view myself this great harmonious oneness of all things, I should stoop to conquer and should hope to succeed by first giving my attention and interest to any matter, tangible or intangible, in earth, air or sea, that he might wish to consider. Nor should I make this a rule merely, nor merely a resort in emergency; I should hold it an ever new, ever old, ever active principle of relation and operation between teacher and pupil. To buy his interest in my themes with my interest in his—always !

For surely the first great step in a teacher's work, every day, every hour, ought to be to find a worthy and practical relationship between the pupil and the thing to be taught. And this may always be found. Of this great creation, nay of such uncreated eternal things as absolute truth also,—of all this harmony of finites and infinites—every human frame and intelligence is a part. Everything in the great entire is somehow each soul's, each body's, affair. Let us, then, labor ever to find out with what things in this great Entire our pupil already feels and enjoys his personal relationship, and bring the things we want to teach him into closer relationship with them. Wherefore let teacher and pupil, like quartermaster and steersman standing at the wheel together, look unceasingly to the practical, personal bearing and result of each lesson, as to a common guiding star.

Men ask, shall we teach the Bible in week-day school? Why not lay the stress on teaching religion, with or without the Bible? Religion will still be in its eternal youth when the Bible has fulfilled its mighty office and passed away from that heaven where there is no temple. Religion is not a knowledge of certain things; it is a state of the heart in which all knowledge should be received and used. How can any good teacher help but teach religion? It is co-extensive with the universe. It is not mere ecclesiastical or academical tenets; it is not any part of life; it is only the whole science and art of life animated and inspired by a universally pervasive and perfect philosophy, the very alphabet of all correct teaching, an alphabet whose Alpha and Omega are Unselfishness.

But unselfishness is not self annihilation nor any effort after it. It is but the subordination of Self to its place in the universal harmony. Its result is—what its motive must never be or the result fails—an immeasurably greater and better aggrandizement of self than any self-seeking can possibly attain. True teaching, then, whether in the Bible or not, can be only that sort which moves the student to ask of every offered acquisition, not, How can this serve Self? but, What self-equipment will this add for that blessed service of the Universal Harmony which by its nature tends to make the whole universe myself and saves me from the folly and ruin of trying to make Self my universe.

With this purpose in view, however we may accomodate ourselves to one pupil's shortness of view or another's narrowness of interest we shall still reflect somewhat of that Light which ever kindly leads toward those great things to the understanding and acceptance of which, as we have said, books and scholarship are but ladders and scaffolding, only aids, however great, and not essentials.

XV.

THE LIVING EPISTLE.

WE have said that to teach the Bible rightly we need, not to teach the Bible, but to use it to teach something yet larger and greater than even the Bible is; that is, christianity as our regular daily business calling. Boys on a training ship are not well taught the compass until the compass is put into practical use to teach them how to steer a ship.

So, Bible teachers, well nigh all the quality of our success depends on how, and how much, we really make the Bible the compass of our life's daily voyage, and how, and how much, we let our pupils find that out. All unconfessed,— even to themselves if they are adults,—that is what they are studying, just in proportion as their minds are bright and their characters above the vice of letting themselves be book-built. You—you—behind your Bible—no matter how constantly you hold it up between you and your pupils—you—however insignificant you try to fancy yourself—you first, and the Bible only afterward and secondarily, are what they are studying. You are the living epistle read of them all. Wherefore modestly, tactfully, constantly, candidly, show them that you recognize and accept this inevitable scrutiny ; seek to multiply your personal relations and experiences with them ; and, teaching always that the Bible is not the daily battle of life, but only the battle-standard, study with them the whole practical art, skill and power of bearing that standard daily and hourly in the fore front.

But you are a busy man or woman ? So much the better ; you are in practice ; you have so many daily practical experiences of life by which to test the moral recipes of the Bible.

But your calling, you insist, is not of a religious character. Then there is something wrong with it ; or, more likely, only with you. Can it be

that you are but an amateur christian ? I have
seen the Bible taught by such ; they taught
nothing, at best, but the Bible, even when they
taught learnedly ; not the things to which the
Bible can only light the way. To teach the
Bible rightly, so that practical christianity shall
be the result, requires not biblical lore, or much
leisure for preparation, or exceptional saintli-
ness ; but that the teacher shall have gone, or is
at least trying to go, professionally into the business of Christ. But the business of Christ em-
braces every business ; every human pursuit
truly tending to advance, not retard, the world's
betterment. Going into christianity professionally does not necessarily change our visible calling, but only its fundamental purposes, the
Master for whom it is performed, and the ends
to which its product is really and unreservedly
dedicated. A man may be a Right Reverend
missionary and not be a professional Christian.
Another may be a professional Christian yet only
saw logs or sell toys if that is the best he can do
to help the world toward the likeness of God.
"God weigheth more with how much love a

man worketh than how much he doeth. He
doeth much that loveth much. He doeth much
that doeth a thing well." So, though you but
hew wood and draw water with the spread of
Christianity for your labor's determined end and
watching with humble eagerness for promotion
along that line, you are already, here and now,
a king and priest unto God. You are showing
the best part of how to teach the Bible. You
have found the true way of life in the true way
to live. Take your Bible, busy Christian and,
with it, teach that. You may be no more than
a good fisherman, but "Thou shalt catch men."